"*Unease at Rest* will hold your hand as the glass shatters. [illegible] comfortable color in the good bruise. Gibson walks you through that tipped trailer to show you where he buries his words. I've discovered a lot of mine there too. This collection will find you only when you need it most."

- Beau Williams
author of *RUMHAM* and *Nail Gun and a Love Letter*

"Wil Gibson's *Unease at Rest* is what poetry was always meant to be- biting, ragged, funny, soothing, undermining, and so real you are changed for having read it. On poem one, I whispered fuck and knew I wouldn't breath again until I had finished the entire book. I'm not sure I survived "Unease" intact. Following the internal terrain of a brilliant mind through the geographical and emotional spaces that haunt and formulate this work left me shifted in place. You are guided kindly and irrevocably to the end, yet still left wondering how you got there. *Unease at Rest* lingers, and you will read it again and again."

- Courtney Butler
author of *Wild Horses*

"Wil Gibson knows his way around the darkest corners of his country, of the human heart, of his own memory. And in his latest collection, he's as fearless as ever in using the fire of his work to shine a light into those places. But there's a greater sense of time in these poems, as if the hardest corners of his own perception have been both softened and focused by his experience. You get the sense that he's looking more at what he's moved through than what he's moving against. There's a sense of peace in that, of rest, and even of forgiveness, however uneasy the road there might have been."

- Nick Fox

POEMS IN THIS COLLECTION
HAVE APPEARED PREVIOUSLY,
SOME IN EARLIER FORMS, WITH:

Drunk in a Midnight Choir
minor literature(s)
Opus Lit
Barking Sycamores
Marsh Hawk Review
Thoughtcrime Press
Moon Pie Press
Cascadia Rising

Swimming with Elephants
PUBLICATIONS

ISBN: 978-0-9998929-5-4

UNEASE AT REST

UNEASE AT REST

BY

WIL GIBSON

To the memories of my Grandaddy, my HoneySun,

and all those who lived lives we should celebrate.

Street poets are scolded if they grow into anything other than older street poets.

(for Beau Williams)

i.

Future lawyers will pay
and eat anything as long
as F Lee Bailey   talks to
them about how interesting
slimy   things   can be
and how to lie   without
lying, but   it would be in
bad taste   to ask him
about the   whole
OJ Simpson   thing.
They don't   like to talk
about   nasty matters in
expensive   restaurants.

My best friend
taught me that.

My best friend
is a better poet,

person, and friend
than I will ever be.

My best friend once fed
me multiple meals, bought
me many multiples of drinks,
got me work, and bailed me
out of jail inside of one very
long week.

My best friend is still
young enough to
change the world,

and will.
I will
only be
a man,

have tried
to be more
than just that,
will never be

more than just that.
It's just that I know
the loaded gun I was
born with and
have been foolish

with such dangerous weapons.
I am not talking about my penis,
I am talking about the privilege

that comes with my penis.

I have wished I didn't have
my penis, but I have never,
even for a second, wished
I didn't have my privilege.

ii.

Old lawyers know
all the tricks.
Old poets think
they know all
the tricks,

write themselves
fairytale. Forget the
rules of the kingdom
they wrote themselves.
At 39, I am told that I am
too old for "slam poetry,"
too young for "page poetry."

My gray
hair isn't
gray enough

for the academic poets,
too gray for the cadence crowd.

I scream too much tattoo
for the turtlenecks; the stone coasts;

the poets in residence;
the Volvo and Subaru folks.

Too much red pen
for the street corners.

Younger poets
call this a hobby

(this loud talk,
m o v e m e n t,
and no podium)

I cough up a civil war statue.
I understand the metaphor,
don't know which side
that makes me a fighter
for, if I am in the fight,
if this is even a fight at
all, or if I even want to fight
a fight that I know
I can never win.

Table of Contents

Part One.

How I...

PART TWO.

(2-c) The most authentic.

FOR SUSANNA.

THE MOST SUPPORTIVE, LOVING, AND HONEST TEAMMATE
WITHOUT WHOM NONE OF MY WORK WOULD EVER GET DONE.

DON'T ARGUE WITH ME.

I read a poem this morning.
It was short and sweet and
simple like all poems should
be. It didn't ask much of me.
Just that I love it. I did, and
do still. I think I always did.

I thought about you this morning.

PART ONE.

"I really don't know who I am,
but it really doesn't matter."

James Dean

HOW I ...

...WRITE.

It is not easy
to be out of control.
It is hard to hold your mouth
like a heavy object when sand
is the most weightless part of each of us.
I do not say "thou" or "thus" in my everyday speech,
have tried to cram those words into poems as if my poems
were thin plastic grocery sacks waiting to tear and
dump these useless things all over the ground.
My words fall on deaf ears and my own feet
quiet enough not to bother anyone; a
mouse with no muse in the
house of conversation.
I break loud.
An unwanted advance of past
feelings and my usual bent promises.
This time I meant to keep my self worth
in addition to the respect of the other
barkers at this foolish carnival. Loss
of a loved one, no matter how loved, or
how one, leaves a click in your jaw that never stops,
makes a detestable noise each time you
hear the person's name. It will echo through your head
like the broken bone it always was.

...KEEP MY MOUTH SHUT

I didn't sleep next to you last night.

I slept in an impeccably decorated
gay man's impeccably decorated
living room in San Francisco
because I do impossibly cliche things
like become infatuated with strong
women and weak boys, or ask

"is this ok?"

when what I really want to say is,

" I really like holding your hand.
Your skin is like... REALLY soft,
your dimple is a basket of puppies and I want to hug it,
but I don't think
that's physically possible,
So instead, can I kiss you on your marble jawbone,
right below your Catwoman eyes,
but above the sword you keep tucked inside
your cheek, next to the violent candle that is your mouth,
if you're ok with that?"

I grinned, tried to hide my teeth.
My teeth are tombstones.
I wish my teeth were more than

ugly machines. Then I could tell

you that I'm not writing a broken girl poem
because I'm a broken boy, I can't fix anything,

I'm no toolbox or workbench.
I am no needle and thread, I
can not fix your frayed edges,

besides,

I like the way your cloth has torn.

Who says we need fixing anyway?
Let's be broken and revel in our pieces.

Let's be rainwater and mud
on the floor, everyone thinks
we're dirty anyway,
let's prove them right.
Let's be so filthy
they have to wash their hands of us.

I am all sawdust bones ready to mix
with your nitroglycerin skin,

Our wax fuses are
melting fast, let's
let it all burn,
righteously burn.

...MELT

There is a word in her breath that
bleeds a sticky black blood on my

skin. A tar-like resin that coats me.
A cocoon. Inside I am all goo. I wait

to become something with wings
instead of just another ugly insect,

then realize that not all insects are
ugly but all insects do ugly things

at times, like live in New England.

New England is a crowded colony.
Crowded colonies are usually ugly.

There is not enough room in a
crowded colony for things like

beauty. When the humans
start to outnumber insects

everything starts to die, I
know that ruins the metaphor,

it is also extremely fucking true.

She said,
"humans are complicated. Bugs are simple."

I heard,
"humans are complicated bugs, and simple,"

and I fell onto the floor.
All goo and no wings.

...Try and look up.

I see geese flying north,
trying to find formation.
I am not sure if they are
lost or if spring is coming
and they are headed
in the right direction.

My father's CB handle
was Green Gander. I am
sure he thought that was
a clever reference to marijuana.
My father and I both love
the song Family Tradition
and think Hank Williams Jr.
is a talented idiot. The biggest
difference between my father
and I is that he is drunk today
and I might be, or that I have
smoked marijuana today and
he only smoked cigarettes.

My father and I both smoke menthol
cigarettes. My father and I both
wish we could smoke KOOLs,
but they are expensive, so we
smoke cheap menthols and

pretend. My father wishes he
could smoke marijuana today,
but he lives in Arkansas, and that
makes smoking marijuana much
more dangerous for him. My father
drives drunk instead.

My father and I both
loved the woman who
was my mother very much.
As a poet, they tell me
not to use the word very
in the way I did in the
previous sentence. They
tell me there are better,
more colorful ways to say it.
I have said it in this way
because it conveys the simple
ease it was to love this woman,
to love the simple way her diseased
heart kept beating long after it
should have stopped,
or to love her lightning bug
laugh and peach cobbler grin.

I am a goose,
more accurately
a gander identifying goose,
and as such I am trying to
find a formation, not sure

if I am going home the right way,
and spring is coming, or if I am lost.

My father is an orphan,
by the strictest definition
of the word. He became an
orphan as an adult. I am sure
my father will die someday
and leave me an orphan by the
strictest definition of the term. I
will be an adult when this happens.

My father adopted my
mother's father as his own.
I am sure this was to help him
replace my mother, and his
mother, and his father, and
his step father; his step father
was the only real father my
father ever knew as a father.
My father has replaced his own
father with other people's fathers
out of necessity. All of my father's
fathers are now dead. My father is
an orphan by every definition of the term

I have tried to replace
my mother with other
people's mothers and
wives and girlfriends,

and other people's wives
and girlfriends, I have
looked for my mother
in every salty moment
in the last 25 years. I can
remember my mother's
25th birthday. My mother
was 30 when she died. My
mother was 16 when I was
born, I was 13 when she died.
I have lived most of my life
with a dead mother.

The geese gather in
a field near where I

live. They think
we are all home.

...STARVE

I wish writing poems paid my
bills, but the last thing most

people want to do is read someone else's
thoughts, most people have plenty of their

own thoughts, others have more than they
can handle. Poets have more than they can

handle. There are poets who pay bills
with poems. I have been one of them,

most of the time I am not one of them.
I am a secondary tourist attraction. You

will not make a special trip to see me,
but if you are in the area...

I am New Hampshire's "Old Man in the Mountain."
Come see me before I crumble and become just another

pile of rocks. A memory most people only
think of when someone else brings it up.

A bad thought about a good thing.

...HURT

I.

The moment the pain stops I begin to
take it for granted. I like to pretend it
will never come back. It usually returns
sooner than later, more intense than before.

My face falls down and to the right. A melted
grin exposes the black lava rock behind my
skin. I melt more often than not. I will melt
again, will leave broken teeth on sink counters
as gifts to the light, and then let my lip curl
inward in an awkward fall to my tongue. I
pull forward to let the torn flesh from the
jagged peaks attached to my gums.

II.

The back pain is the least important part
of sleeping anywhere they will let you. It
has changed me, sleeping anywhere they will
let me. Bent my body while it heats
my bones. A red hot steel beam most of
my life; I bend easily. If you touch me, you
will melt into me. I will absorb you and become
diluted. There will be no "you" anymore. Just
a part of me. My glow has dimmed. I have
cooled, my spine hardened. I sleep where I am
allowed, these days, but am unable to decide when.

...HAUNT

When you walk in graveyards
do not be surprised when you

see a few corpses. These dead
people you are afraid of are only

what the locals call, "locals." You
are not a local so you call them

ghosts without seeing how dead you
have become. These friends wish to

tear you apart now. Let them tear you
apart now. Become one of them again

until it is time to run again. Always run again.
It is what you do, again. What drives you to

be what you perceive as successful, perceive
yourself as successful even if it isn't success

you want. Want more. Be happy with less.
Work for more back where you run from,

or to, depending on which way you run. These
places you run to or from; these locals you see

as dead; these lies you tell yourself; these forests,
they all drag your feet across the grave you roll over

in, you deadman; you ghost; you broken back; you
lost dog with no collar in the California rain.

...READ

Eyes double
a regular view
world letter a second
magically back, become
angles. My sight changes.
A pair of broken glasses.
My misunderstandings into
the thing by mind shapes my
see jumps absence, order, regulation.
The basis flip twice and forth
opposite to the mental bite,
crumpled the vowels to my confined
sees sometimes nothing but how my
3-D is stolen the only out that ever blink with.

My eyes see double on a regular basis.
I view the world twice a second.
Letters flip magically back and forth
become angles opposite to my
mental misunderstandings, bite
broken vowels into crumpled consonants
confined by how my mind sees shapes sometimes.
Dyslexia is nothing but a broken pair of 3-D glasses.
The only thing jumps out is the absence of order and
regulation. My stolen sight changes with each blink.
Nothing ever stays the same.

...STARE.

I have not seen the last grain of sand
fall through the hourglass today.
It must have, I just didn't see it fall.

My favorite colors have always been
a palate of ideas. Orange and brown
appeal to me most of the time, but
purple and black are family.

My explanations.

By that I mean they explain
my tooth fairy personality.

I want to give people things for the
pieces of themselves that they let me
have. I will give them more now than
I did when I was younger. It still will
not be enough, in comparison, I am a
negative number, a loss. I try to add

something.

...GOT GOT.

"No one saw me doing this
People can't decide how they're viewing this."
~G.E. Gillum

In the back of the bus I listened
to their odd new-friend conversation
about cooking steak,
like it matters how
steak is cooked.
It does not matter.
It was a stale coffee taste on the
end of a greasy diner breakfast.
They both tasted bad but I expected
nothing less from the cook and server.
They were the last strangers I will talk to for 3 days.
They made me talk to them.
I amplified the music in my headphones
and watched their lips move. They flirted
and made eyes and I may have been projecting
that because I was about to see my girlfriend
for the first time in two months, but they
would make a cute couple anyway.
The cook and the server are
not a cook and a server,
they are drunk. Loud and
laughing from the 2 bottles
of wine they have had in 4
hours in the belly of this

white whale of an Amtrak bus.
A bus that is definitely a cover for
smuggling weed to and from Humboldt.

I love living in California.

I had weed delivered to me at the
train station during a 45 minute
transfer/layover. At the transfer
Amtrak turned into a bus which
had nothing to do with the weed.
It was a very nice bus, shared
by the cook and server and me and
5 or 6 other people going to the
greenest place on the planet.
The driver didn't care that we all
smoked a blunt at the meal stop.
The driver didn't give a fuck about anything.
He left early, skipped stops if he
thought no one was there, and took
corners at speeds ill-suited for
mountain traffic. Never mind the
bounce of the entire vehicle when
the fractured asphalt became a minefield.
I listened to highway under the train
that was actually a bus and then made
fun of myself being cliché and then make
fun of clichés. I like clichés. They feel
like I do after a job interview that went well
for a job I know that I will not get.

...WROTE.

Today I will receive the first copies
of a new book of poems I have written.

I began writing these poems on the sightseeing
car aboard an Amtrak train that howled east across

the Sierra Nevada mountains. The first poems I wrote
were about my family dying off like the insects that we are.

In this book, I made reference
to myself as a ghost

several times, and that might

have been the truest things
I have ever written.

In this book, I fell in and out of love

with a barbed wire fence at least three times,
fell a little bit out of love with a teardrop tattoo once.

In this book, I quit killing myself slowly
with smoke and started the fire again.

I also quit smoking cigarettes.

In this book, I bent my heart
over the edge of a cliff

carved by the kind of
giant Gods that are

active in people's lives
day to day, rung my

weird heart over wood pulp
as a penance for my, and others'

sins. Several characters in
this book of poems were

portrayed so accurately that
they will never speak to me again.

Today, I will begin my next
book of reasons why someone else

will never speak to me again.

PART TWO.

"We kill all the caterpillars and complain there are no butterflies."

John Marsden

THE SOFTEST WINGS

There is no way for me to be
uncomfortable for someone
without showing it.

Myself,

I change

position
in my seat,

or

Step
on
my
own
feet.

A small way to cope
with my discomfort for others

is to make myself
physically
uncomfortable.

I know that this
    does not help them,
does not make   them feel better.

My lack of physical comfort
makes me more comfortable.

Movement is my comfort,
I suffer   from an
"unease at rest,"

    find odd comfort in the
quiet afforded by

physical
        white noise.

This silence is not awkward;
feels

honest,
as

the moment
just after
a car crash,

or

the   one   just   as

someone has begun
to die, and also after.
The strange beautiful tinge
of blue that their skin turns when
they stop
being able
to
breathe.

The instant a

newborn deer
walks,

or an ugly butterfly
u n f u r l s
itself. Those

soft, awkward, and
most authentic wings.

(2-A) SOFT.

EUREKA.

She has fog smooth skin
and a razor blade for a
left front tooth. Tells me

she doesn't know what she
deserves when it is obvious
that she made the moon stick

to the sky and turned stars into
freckles. She says she wishes
the freckles were gone, that its

too expensive to have the stars removed,
openly admits to being afraid of being cut
open again, that childbirth left scars she is

ashamed of. Calls me sugar, I think of
rotted teeth and diabetes, says sweet
things. I am too much missing and not

enough home-cooked meals. She thinks
I'm front porch sweet tea, but doesn't taste
the bitter root of the kudzu vines or the

burning snow in my throat. I want so
much more than the ocean and all the

fish in it. More than the microwave s'mores,

dandelion whisky nights and misfit
sweat-soaked mornings. She resurrects
people for a living and doesn't see my

grim dead moments. There are steel beams
in her fingers and a fire in her feet. There are
gold rings melted into the floor that we both

try not to notice. Six of them. We want to
scrape them up and melt us all together.
There are times to stuff family into caskets

that save lives. Secret little tricks that
fool and educate. I want to learn how
to be happy. I want to know what

happy looks like in the morning. I have
never been happy in the morning. I have
often had trouble with a smile when the

sun is up. I wanted to end this poem
with a metaphor about darkness to
contrast all of this light that she is,

because in the light I am afraid she
will see too much and be afraid of
my dumb ol' black broken heart.

Landslide.

I.

Her skin
(smooth, soft as rabbit fur)
slid against mine
(calloused, torn as a bedsheet).

She said
(lips and words brushed my ear),
I like you
(disappointment and a deadline in her voice).

II.

It isn't easy
to be used by people.
It isn't easy
to have used people.

It is far easier
to be in bloom
or to have bloomed.

Everything beautiful is dangerous.

(after "Medusa Gets a Booty Call" by Adrienne Nadeau)

I walked the sea snakes from
around my legs. Smashed my
feet over rocks that looked like
familiar faces and others

that looked like mirrors. The stories
were never more than symbols to me,
analogies that forced my legs to shake

while they could. I crawled on ships, walked
tall across cobblestones. I have bled through
enough open wounds to see that sand is just

a series of very small stones that collect together
in an attempt to rebuild themselves into mountains.

They were parts of a
mountain at one time,
just wind blown dunes now.

She doesn't have all the
powers people have given
her in stories. Her strength
comes more from the curve
of our hearts and the curve of
her Earth than her eyes. She

locks you in with her landscape,
her eyes seal your fate.

We all fall in love with her.
That's the part of the myth
everyone seems to forget.

We do this to ourselves, to be
what she wants--be it rock, skin, stones,
or flesh. If she wants to watch us crumble,
she only has to push us away, our legs can't

walk away ever again. We will tip
over, stiff and rigid as eternity. This
is how we wait for her

to want us again.

I thought I was different.
That she shattered me by accident,
was too stuck in the cycle
of serendipity and statue.

I assumed she tried to
save me when she told me
not to see who she really was,
warned me that most men are
the same, they crumble, no stone
lasts forever, man and sand is just
small stones trying to be bigger than

they are, we freeze and crack, or split.

When she looked at me, what I saw
was no magic. The snakes aren't all
snakes. She doesn't really turn you
into stone. Her cement mixing soul
pours a mold of you. She keeps that,
cherishes the memory of each suitor
like a birthday card. She is a talented

stonecutter, an artisan that shows
us who we really are. A woman of
power is the most frightening thing
in the world to weak men. Leaves
them stunned. Stone silent.

I went away, spread myself across
beaches where there was bloodshed,

with the hope that being a battlefield would stop me
from becoming a fallen pile of stone,
the guts of an hourglass, sand that soaks up
the blood from this holy beachhead.
I wash in and out in vain with waves, more mud than rock.

I wish she would walk on me.
Wish she could hear me say,
"I am sorry I was not strong enough
to love you without falling apart."

Nay.

The curve of her hips was
a quiet roller coaster. My
hands slid along the tracks,
hushed at every drop and
dip, never let go of the safety
bar. We were not the least bit
slow. Not even during the climb.
The roll of the metal along the
swoop and bend washed away
all the silence. We all heard the
scream. I bent my arm around
her bed, became the monster we
all fear that we are becoming.

I have not lied to someone to get them
to sleep with me in a very long time.
I am aware that some people will
not listen to the truth, will hear
what they wish, will believe their
own wants over my words. I used to
be something more villain, less often
mistaken, clumsy fool. I am aware of my
loneliness, these days, act less bullfrog
and more spun gold. Will still turn skin green.
A stain that won't wash away;
bloodstains on the barn wall;
piss stains on torn sheets;

gold stains on the mountainside;
vomit stains under a roller coaster;
the worst part of any beautiful moment.

FIRST WE DANCED.

The last time she was more
than a one night stand was
just after me. We spent one night

standing on the edge of her bed
like a cliff. Too drunk to be
anything other than warm bodies.

It can't be a one night stand if
we have been waiting eight years
for the chance to be alone. She held
me crossroad and I helped her out of
her cracked shell. She is too powerful

for her own good, too small to be anything
but a target, assumes everyone wants to take

their shot. She lay on me, touched a fantasy
while I melted into the black sheets under us.

There was so much sad in her laugh
that it scared us both. I drank her wine,
held her body across my battleline skin

and wondered how something so broken

could be so soft. I asked her if I was a traitor,

she told me I had no countries to swear to.
I wanted to help feed the smallest side of her,
never saw more than the back of her head,
never let herself look me in the eye.

Remora.

The film of grit
across the table
is from the food
I have cooked
for a family I am
part of in presence
I am not bound by
blood here I stick myself
to them to survive I eat what
is left while I burn my body then

pile myself into the darkest
corner

where I try to stay out of the way.

To those who won't walk over subway grates.

I used to be younger.

Back then I died a lot.

Now I fear it less,

D E A T H,

am more conscious
of my   actions

I don't sniff fairy dust
anymore. My   Peter
Pan past left me more
Captain Hook these days
(ya know-I chase monsters,
clocks scare me-I'm told I
forget how easy it is to fly).

I had
forgotten
that   being
stuck
is more about   being

patient,
moving slowly,
breathing.
That this is what sets you free;
that frantic movement   only
gets you   more stuck.

I used to be younger.

Back then I lived as much
as I do now,   but I did
all of the   drugs I could
and tried to   kill myself
a large   family   of   times.

It was difficult to find the time
to do both   of those things.

I managed to find the time
to do   both of those things

and walk more than   half of
this continent. I wish I could
remember more of it but my
memory is a trailer park that
I   k n o w   I
should   stop writing about.

This   morning
I put too much

sugar   in my
coffin   watch
these   bones
shake.

When my phone vibrates,
I know it will be one of a few people.
When it isn't you, it is a swollen fist,
when it is a swollen fist, your eyes soften.
Thank you for having soft eyes.

Teach me about trees.
Show me how
they grow.
Show me how trees move.
Show me where they
are trying to get.

Tell me about the moment you
stopped walking over subway grates,
why you say you do it because you're
afraid of other people's mistakes.

I stomp over subway grates,
manhole covers, and street doors
when we are together and say I do it
because I like fucking with you,
but the real reason
is when I'm alone

I walk around them too.

I'm too afraid to be
brave without an audience.

I guess it makes sense that
we pour blood on strangers
and call it entertainment.

Everyone   wants to see
bravery and blood on display,

some are just   more
violent about it than others.

I used to be younger.

Back then I died a lot.

I have runaway issues
and worship strange
gods. These gods tell
me I am not worthy,

that I don't matter enough
to stay anywhere too long,

that my existence is
cumbersome, wasteful,

that people are lying to me
when they say that they love me.

My gods tell me that
love and pity are so similar
that they fool even the brightest minds.

Makes me pray on my knees
most morning just to be able
to face the day's failed   try.

Has my
strange heart near explosion
when I try to force sleep and
remember the day's current failed try.

I used to be younger.

Back then I just   died
whenever the thick grey sky
pulled in too   close for me
to see   my way out.

Cut ties with the world
any chance I got. Lost
moments and memories
and people so I would
feel less like a burden.

I don't feel like a burden

here,   in these words.

I feel   useful,
I like feeling useful.

I feel   brave.
I like feeling brave
(even if it is just
for an audience).

I feel   young,
I like feeling young.

I don't want to die.
I'm too old to   die
              anymore.

(2-B) AWKWARD.

It was Thursday morning.

When there are doubts
about self-worth in the
most star-crossed moments,
to suffer is to prosper.

While that sounds like
some Buddhist shit, and
probably is, the modern
equivalent is to be arrested
in the middle of a high school residency
for a fine you have been paying on for three years,
paying little by little when you had the money,
apparently not enough to stave off warrants,
in front of students,
in front of your little brother,
in front of teachers you respect,

or maybe the modern equivalent
is to be forced to sit on a stack
of your most embarrassing poems
and explain your poor judgements
to a jury of your students and literary heroes.

It was Thursday night.

She shook under me

like the world was

moving. It wasn't.

We smash our

skin

together

like a car crash.

We are wasteful.

(for John W. Simpson)

I have watched my family die from their
own ignorance and lack of health care.
These are similar things in some areas of
this vast country. My family and myself
suffer this sin with a toothless grin. We
are used to this type of life, with all this
young death. We are an uneasy people,
rounded like Crowley's Ridge and jagged
as the Vicksburg Cliffs. This is the reason
for all this proud ignorance and near constant
state of rebellion in some foul fashion: we see
ourselves as the good guys in black, the world
sees us as the dirty bad guys in white, destined
to fail. We will know nothing else except this loose
hope, this bent edition of a beautiful, unattainable dream.

AGAIN.

Every word I hear
from the police
in press releases
sounds like a gun
being reloaded.

I know why
I know who
will
shoot next,
who
will
shoot first.

Six on seven of eight.

(for Nick Fox)

i.

She said The only way out is south and
I tried to pretend it was a metaphor not a
factual statement. I am uncomfortable with
these kinds of factual statements that work
as well or better when used as metaphors.

ii.

Poets are lazy novelists who cut
themselves short and make the reader
tell the story on their own. Novelists
are lazy poets who over explain the
story and say *and, so, but, and because*
too much. I could have just said poets
are lazy novelists and novelists are poets,
but I am a lazy poet who says and, *so,*
but, and because too much.

iii.

I am told that short story writers

are patient people. That seems like
a contradiction, although, I am not
a good short story writer or a good
patient people, so maybe I just do
not have accurate information

iv.

I used to think that some people
spelled their names oddly, but it is their
name, so they can spell it however they
wish. Today I met a person named Craig.
It was spelled with a Y... like Crayg.
No.
Just.
No.

v.

The last time I remember truly
liking myself, each poem I wrote
was a limp branch over a dusty old
Oklahoma red dirt driveway. The
branches broke like the storm did.
I got to the end of the road before
the last Lacebark Elm died. The

dried leaves fell like dried tears.
I have not stopped moving since
the limbs snapped. I make jokes
in the face of these thunderstorms
that roll after me like a wave of nausea.

vi.

When some snakes swallow, they
stare directly up and then wiggle the
food down to make sure they do not
choke. After that they don't eat again
for up to four entire weeks. I am still
uncomfortable with these kinds of
factual statements that work as well
or better when used as metaphors.

Pulse

I listened to the soft racism
in the booth next to me. Heard
it spread across the room,

become sexist and then
homophobic before it rested
at my foot. Western Colorado

is not all that unlike Utah, or Texas,
or Alabama; all places that pretend
to be different but hold the same

loose truths to be self-evident.
The fast accents are not as adorable,
the hate here is funny to the locals.

On this sunday, we had just found out
another shooting had happened, this
shooting in Florida, the same town

where a fan shot a pop singer
after her concert less than
24 hours earlier. This shooting

has left more than twice that many
dead and a whole country injured.
At first, these old cowboys seemed

concerned. When it was revealed
that this happened at a gay club,
the concern became attempt at

comedy, too many jokes to give
one as an example. My stomach
turned from sadness and anger

and I realized this small, fruit-filled
town surrounded by so many kinds
of fossils would be where the last tree dies.

Night Sweats

We drank till we had
no options for escape then
ran away anyway,
had spent all energy

on wishes to be somewhere
less like the movies. We
know our place in the
movies. We are not the

main characters. We are the
plucky best friends, the bad
guys because of where we
live but by the end of the movie

you've come to see that we
ain't so bad after all, but are
still the antagonists. In these
movies we are not protectors,

we are always depicted as the
aggressors. We are greasers and
greasy. No matter the reality,

we will always be seen as the

problem. The ones who escalate
tense situations. Wolves that howl

at the moon,
slammed car doors,
and scars. The ominous
figure in the corner, cornered.

WHY EDWARD KENNEDY WAS FORGIVEN FOR THE TIME HE DROVE HIS OLDSMOBILE INTO A POND

(AFTER RICHARD KRECH)

The poppies that they gather
only grow in blood soaked soil
under dark mountain ranges. Every
thing crumbles under the weight of
these white washed walls and
burned history books.

No one remembers the call girl's names
and the public easily forgives a rapist.

The television allows you
to alter the way you see the
world, and the time, has a
specific menu for those things,
all starts with the buttons you push.

Wal-Mart sells thousands
of them a year, claims not
to know the difference
between black and white TVs
or what used to be called,

"color TVs" that we now call
"smart TVs", and we never
even had a parade. Nothing to

suggest the change was important
enough to be recollected or reelected,
while the proof of these roses and all
other flowers still stained his chalky hands.

I DON'T KNOW WHAT TO DO.

The limit of color is a vacuum sealed secret. The lighter the pigment, the darker the past actions, or so it seems. The skin reflects the opposite angles of these better angels we try to nurture in the cracked spines we let serve as our backbones. We have lost our empty backbones, too afraid of being treated as we have treated. Afraid. Scared to face the earned consequences of past ancestry because we should be. We should be.

On Flying Over Mt. Shasta

The snow is more visible
from above it. There is more

snow than you can see from
the ground. Not only because
you can see all the way around

the jagged peak to the valley that
adds height to the rock by
sub-
tract-
ing itself,
also because the

view from below looks

smaller

if you are further away. This
is how perspective works.

Humans think they
can work perspective,

bend it to whatever flawed red thoughts

they award value.
From thirty thousand feet
above
                    the

ground,

perspective is skewed to shrink
even the largest mountains

into stomped anthills;
sand castles
that wash away
at high tide.

I am not sure
when high tide
is coming.
Christians say
it will come soon.

As a Jew,
I am told
the world

has ended before,
will end again,
has always ended.

I may be confusing the text,
or mistaking what you may
think of as
The Old Testament
for the book
"Slaughterhouse-5"
by Kurt Vonnegut,
which is my all-time
favorite book.

I do not think either book
has more merit than the other,
or that either is the word of God.
I am told both books have been
banned at some point in the past,
along with "Huck Finn" and the Koran.

Religious books do not get
quotation marks or italics
around them because they
are loaded with other things
like plasma and suffering.

Mt. Shasta has killed hikers at a
less dangerous level than most
religious texts. I am sure there
are warning signs all around
Mt. Shasta cautioning people
to the dangers of bears,
mountain lions, falling trees,
invasive plants, and more.

I am positive that Billy Pilgrim
is a figment of Mr. Vonnegut's
imagination. There is no warning
to the dangers
of reading
too faithfully
when concerning
fiction and even
less still with nonfiction.

It is assumed
that some things
are just stories
to entertain, and
others are
to enlighten,
to teach.

(2-C) The most authentic.

THE SPRAYPAINT SMILE ON THE BRIDGE IS FAKE.

(A POEM FOR WYNNE, AND ALL OF EASTERN ARKANSAS; AFTER C.L. BLEDSOE)

There are bank parking lots full of
kids with Papaw's truck that is
covered in Confederate flags.
They drive up to Sonic and park
and drive back to the bank
to park again. They yell about
black people like dogs barking
after a pedestrian that has
never even come close to its yard.

They yip, and growl, and curl lips,
all full of tobacco spit and Daddy's
drunken rants and none of them
have ever seen an ocean. Never
thought to go see one. They don't
dream that big. There are bushels
of skeletons that block the street,
that block everyone from getting
out. There is a 90 year old mattress
in Grandaddy's trailer that 3 family
members have died on. People have
fallen in love and hearts have been
broken all around that mattress. There
are secrets behind the brick homes up
on the ridge and love in the trailer parks.

Across the street from the trailer park is
a middle school. Behind that middle school
is a spot under a tree where too many locals
have lost their virginity. There is still blood on
the ground in that spot. There are houses with
dirt floors and toothless women at the kitchen
table with bald, dying old men out in the yard
that yell in to the women at the table. They say,

"I Love ya, ya fat old bitch,"

and they mean every single word. They do
not see the problems. The problems that rise from
the greenish smoke, angry little people who cook
magic powders and choke the life out of the bored
locals. Everyone gags on something. There are limits,
not only on the bullet hole covered signs. The speed
leaks off the 3 bloated new downtown buildings and

drive thru liquor stores.
(THERE ARE DRIVE THRU LIQUOR STORES!)

Booze and the perception of movement
are the only options, but Little Rock
is scary and Forrest City is a big city
of 13,000 people if you could count
all the illegal farm workers. There are
drugs everywhere and nowhere and
all places in between. Evil hides in
quiet corners and in only God can judge me

smirks as it judges you from the front
church pew and tries to fight you in the
parking lot. There are issues unresolved
floating in the Walmart aisles where
shoppers mock each other after they
pass, always under their breath. No one
wants confrontation in such a holy place.
There are train tracks that still divide
the town along color lines. The whites
call the black side of town "Colored Town"
like their great-grandfathers did, and
hate those of us who ignore the
borders with a smile. There are places
that surround this little rice and cotton
cluster where they warn black people
to get out by sundown, and they do.
There are towns that warn white people
to get out by sundown, and they do,

(THERE ARE SUNDOWN TOWNS!)

There are rules here.
There are questions that
linger on tongues, but never
find the courage to come out
into the humid air, and dry
answers that no one seems to have
or want to share. Everyone knows
where McDonald's is, knows that
Hays and Wal-Mart switched spots,

that Burger King closed, and Sonic
crossed the street, but they can't give
you directions to the library because

"it closed last year, ain't it?"

The willful ignorance soaks through
the street like a flood no one cares to stop.
They will drown here someday.
No one will learn to swim.

His eyes were sharp as a Sunday suit.

The sweat rolled to his elbow. Paused
for effect at the point and dripped slow
as night to the ground. This happened
every few minutes, then every few seconds,
then became a steady drip...drip...drip...drip.

When the salty water fell, the earth shook beneath
his feet with a thunder gods get jealous of, but all
gods are angry or jealous. He never really liked this
kind of work. Too forced; too fake. His hands were
the size of full lunchboxes, heavy as third grade textbooks.

He was more than human or animal of any kind. He
stopped short of talking several times. Held his words
like the coffee mug or the cigarette in his hands at
breaktime. He was all bent from the bottom up,
broken from his chest to his neck. His back was
weak, but hadn't busted yet. Everyone has always
thought he was so strong.

He couldn't remember the last time he read anything
other than an instruction manual, knew it had something
to do with passion. Couldn't remember where he put the
book, says it must have burned up when he still had some
fire in his belly. Hadn't seen any book in years. He
remembered

every book he had ever read, but couldn't recall who wrote it.

"I only read the one, something about rats or mice, and how men think killing can be compassionate. I didn't like the way it sat in my stomach," he said, "so I didn't bother to do it again."

FOR THE TWEAKERS ABOUT TO STOP USING.

The burnt snow smell
and chemical stench
sticks to your clothes
a little bit less than it
sticks to the smoldering
wreckage of your memory.

You will still recognize
the scent of a good cook
even after you haven't eaten
their powdered meals in over
a decade. The green mists you
see rising up from those hidden
kitchens will always make you itch.

Your teeth will not hurt
for the rest of your life.
They will eventually fall out
or crumble and become
spear point reminders to
make friends with a good
dentist as soon as possible.

The pain of every cold breeze will
cut your gums like a gutter-found razor.
Anything other than room temperature

in your mouth will be like chewing thorn
bush bites into small indigestible pieces.

You will gain 50 pounds in a week,
and though you have lost more in
less time, this time your body will turn
against you and inside of itself. Your skin
will become impacted with every atom of
the poison you have stuffed into your body.

Your stomach will bleed as it peels layer
after layer off like the scab you have become,
and lets your bowels make you an unwitting
cannibal. You will eat yourself sober and lose
chunks of your intestines to the roller coaster
of diarrhea and constipation that will start to run
your life like the drug you have stopped taking
but hasn't stopped taking from you. You will never
shit properly again...EVER.

Your family will not know how
to talk to you anymore, if they
talk to you at all. They will smile
a wounded animal at you when
they see you because they are
animals and you have wounded them.

The time it takes you to physically forget
that you used to use meth
will be half as long as it takes

for them to pretend to forget
that you used to use meth.
They will never forget
that you used to use meth.
They will be almost as afraid
of the past as you will be.
It will seem like distrust.
It is fear. Let them fear you,
they have seen you at your worst.
They expect your worst now.

What you have done to yourself
might be the worst thing that
has ever happened to them.

After a honeymoon of comas,
sleep will run from you again.
Your conscious will taunt you,
each night will haunt you
like a disappointed mother.
More than 3 hours of consecutive
rest will seem less than possible.
Sunrise will wake you.
Crickets will wake you.
Slight breezes will wake you.
The car door closing blocks away will wake you.
The blink of every star will be
a cymbal crash symphony in the silence.
Sound sleep will be a dream
you may never see again.

Never mind the nightmares.

The sunset will not be as beautiful as you remember.
The colors will be as bland and lifeless as a badly cut
construction paper heart on a classroom wall.

Most things will seem Mudville joyless. You will think
you have used all the happiness allotted to a lifetime.
Every smile will seem a lie. Every laugh will feel forced.

Society will see all of this on you when they look at you.
They will smell four a.m. on your flesh and turn their noses
at the stench. You will represent every part of poverty and
poor choices that they are uncomfortable with. They will
loath you for that and judge you more harshly than any
jury of your peers. All you can do is give them new
reasons to see you as something less insignificant,
more survivor, less extinct. Those moments will
present themselves. You won't see them until
you train yourself to seem well adjusted.
You will never be well adjusted.
You might as well adjust.

Quitting meth will be the hardest,
most thankless thing that you will ever do.

It is worth it.

SEE ME POET.

I watched soft brown and pink faces
wander among the hard red and brown rocks.

Mothers held hands with daughters.
Husbands raced sons around trails.
Couples kissed in full view of us all.

I wandered too.

I, alone,
my children
in 3 separate
states, none of them near
the one I stand in.

All of them various degrees
of hurt, angry, or confused.

By me.

By my various degrees
of hurt, anger, and confusion;

by my various degrees of
movement (mostly away).

I am confused by my hurt and anger;
confused by all this need for movement.

I do not know why I love these highways,
these people I have yet to meet.

I do not know the reason
for all these four in the mornings,
and bad parental choices.

I only think that they need me.

I do not think I need them.
I need love, like all live things.

Love has been too many
metaphors
for life, for light,
for my own fragile ego.

I am in search of just one that makes sense.

The best analogies ever written are:

Life IS...
Love IS...
You ARE
We ARE...
I AM...

We poets only think we can do better while we
smash our faces into our little paper walls, hold our
feet to the ground like we don't know that we are
weightless, we poets. We are too heavy for all these
weak measurements. I am a weak measurement
of a poet, of what I think a poet is supposed to be.

See me metaphor poorly.
See me too many/too few/too obscure/too long/too short/too
    dumb/too easy analogy.
See me poet
and poet
and poet some again.

See me wonder why no one likes me.
See me know my poems are terrible.
See me write them anyway and
wonder why no one likes my terrible poems.

See me poet.

See me go to jail.
See me write poems about going to jail.
See me go cross country for no reason.
See me look for reasons.
See me look.
See me suicide.

See me poet.

See me never talk to family and
friends because I am always gone.
See me lose family and friends
because they got used to
me always being gone.

See me poet and poet and poet again

See me cry alone after a show that doesn't go well.
See me celebrate too much when a show does go well.
See me scream at nothing because a promoter didn't
pay the promised and I don't know anyone for 100 miles.
See me not mention any names because some of y'all
might go to U of Maine Presque Isle or
know who the fuck Mike Guinn and Aaron Dockard are.

See me cry alone after the best show of my life.
See me have those moments to myself.
See me be by myself in those moments.
See me touch hearts but only hug bodies.
See me want to touch so bad it hurts.
See me want to be touched so bad it hurts.
See me want to touch bodies so badly that it hurts my heart.
See me only get flirted with when I do memorized poems.
See me never know when I'm getting flirted with
and hate my memorized poems.

See me poet and poet and poet some more.

See me write, fail,

read, drink, cuss,
fuck, want, wish,
lust, shine, smoke,
see me fade,
see me die,
see me poet.

TRUE STORIES.

When I was 10 I had this friend that everyone looked up to a lot, but whenever we were around each other we did the dumbest shit and always got caught. I remember once him trying to dive out my bathroom window because my Mama was gonna whoop his ass. I was on the outside so all I saw was his terrified face as she pulled him in and away from me. I haven't seen him in 20 years. *(you and he have the same color hair)* When I was 15, I was seeing this girl my father had forbidden me from being with. I called her and said "leave your front door unlocked. I'll be there as soon as my father leaves for his eleven o'clock- twelve hour -third shift." As I was making my way across town a police woman stopped me to see where I was supposed to be. I gave my girlfriend's address as my own and watched as that tough-as-nails officer turned mother figure right in front of my eyes and gave me a ride the rest of the way. My first booty call had a police escort. *(you and that cop have the same sweet face)* When I was 13, my mom was dying. Waiting to be unplugged like a broken TV set, all the color and pictures now gone. She couldn't move. All I could do was stare at her purple swollen body through double paned Loyola ICU glass. A nurse noticed my anguish and said "Hey kid, let me show you something I bet you don't know. Today, at sunset, your mom will make the entire city of Chicago turn gold." I followed him to the sixth floor of stairwell nine. We could see the entire skyline. He said, "Close your eyes, and think of your favorite memory with your mother." As I did, the sun sank behind us in the west, when I opened my eyes the city glowed like a jagged golden moon and I knew that my Mama had made it for me...at least on that day. On my way back to the waiting room we had made into our impromtu home, I noticed the chapel, and ducked inside. Seeing no one, I began to pray out loud. I prayed as long and as hard as a thirteen-year-old can, which is way harder than any adult can. I tried to tell god all the reasons I should be able to keep my mother. You can't rationalize with god. I begged god to let me keep her. God doesn't answer beggars. Leaving, I saw the same nurse in the back pew, still smiling. (*you and that nurse have the same soft smile)* I haven't prayed much since that day, but for some reason I like unanswered prayers. Silent, unspoken, personal wishes. Some sunsets come at midnight, others come at noon, and some give cities a golden heaven-sent hue. That's what they're supposed to do. All of you are someone's sunset, and for that, thank you.

BLOOD.

Can scatter like
sand to the wind
and still be a part
of the same polluted
beach; the same untilled
ground; the same soft pillow
moved from bed to bed to bed
each time your address changes,
each time your address changes it
follows in your skin; is your skin.

Lindsey.

Climbing each step to a mountaintop that
isn't there, is a test of your bravery and
willingness to be a small speck on a large rock.

(We are all small specks on a large rock.)

At the top, see the half-bubble sky full of stars that
are too far apart to be a universe yet are somehow
a collection of all the same cliché stardust that sits
in my stomach, in yours.

Savannah.

Our self-worth can not
be found in anyone's
eyes but our own.

We stare through the fog
we surround ourselves with,
wipe away positive thought like
steam on a mirror, watch ourselves
run down the glass like rivers of doubt,
drip soft in a puddle on the floor that we
wet feet in, unwillingly, until the moisture dries.
The moisture always dries.

In West Texas,

the wind never
stops blowing,
hums a melody
under your door
at night, sings a
tune you forgot
that you loved.

The whistle of this
natural music is
the inspiration
for a thousand
songs a year.

We sing.

The latest lost
loved one leaves
a bitter taste
on the tongue,
whisper inside
ourselves, a lonely
sound. The hills try
to hide, are almost gone.

TO THE STUDENT WHO ASKED ME HOW TO BE A WRITER.

(((EDIT))) Forget everything ever written. Better still (((READ))) everything ever written and edit out the mistakes. Fix them with every pen stroke of your imagination (((SHOW US WHAT WE HAVE DONE WRONG))) Pretend the devil is a poem that revised itself without a sound. An antic of the mind. A flickering fairy made up of the same self doubt you force yourself to breathe then rattle off long windblown rants about bad drivers, your mother, local sports teams, or Rc Cola whinos (((JUST MAKE SOME SHIT UP))) If the truth is blue (((BE BLUE))) write all over yourself with bright yellow ink see what color reality shines through with fight crows, be falcon, fight falcon, be eagle, be open to fail, (((YOU GONNA FAIL))) (((YOU WILL SUCCEED))) (((NEITHER WILL MATTER IF YOU DON'T LOVE YOUR IMPERFECTIONS))) Remember the mouth of the first boy, girl, or non gender specific person who ever called you cute. (((IF NO ONE HAS EVER CALLED YOU CUTE BEFORE, YOU ARE CUTE.))) Be the swarm of bees in a '37 ford just outside of Memphis. Be cracked engine block. Be broken odometer. Be forty years of rust around you, now dust it all off and open the throttle to ninety on a back road in Bald Knob, Arkansas in December of 1938. Be every road pebble click against your tires, explode. (((KEEP WRITING))) Be as beautiful and as quick as death. Own your evils in a world short on flowers. Tell us slow, the mother-in-law drowning in her grocery cart, the son-in-law smoking pot in the parking lot exhaling white hot excuses. Lie about liking

Ramen noodles. (((YOU WILL HAVE TO))) Be the broken, be the glue snap the blank page's tooth. Liberate all the abandoned engagement rings from all the pawn shops. Make mad rants about the couple arguing in the middle of the million dollar bridge. Write your name gently on the first green leaf in spring then be angry and amazed every autumn when it's not stuck to the window of your first car. Stab hearts with notebooks and microphones. Sharpen them. As blunt objects, they only bruise, they don't cut through, they don't break. Imagine God in your strong hand. She rests until lightning crashes simile in your palm and poetic device in your spleen, until eyes open like pickle jars and lips part singing sober heart murmur. Televise your revolution, better still (((TWEET))) your revolution. That's the only way it will be seen. (((IN FIVE YEARS ALL OF THIS ADVICE WILL BE OBSOLETE ---I'M SORRY--- EDIT IT))) Edit our mistakes with your smiles, your strengths, your weaknesses, yourselves, your poems, (((EDIT THE WORLD))) (((EDITeditEDIT editEDITeditEDITeditEDITeditEDITeditEDit)))

Arkansas is a Graveyard.

My boots leave small

gravestone marker shapes

behind me.

They hold ever so slightly

in the Mississippi River mud

until they snap back to my heel.

When I look back

I can see the carnage

I have created.

A bulldog named Brutus.

When I was a child,
my cold winter breath

was the smoke from
an imaginary cigarette.

Now, I write walls around myself
until I'm trapped, coat my lungs

with tar and feathers, and
breathe fire on my students.

Hypocrisy is rarely seen by a hypocrite.

My mother is sleeping. Still.
Has no breath

in someone else's lungs.
Her heart was thrown aside,

over used. Doctors replaced
it with a heart from an old man

for just three days, then was taken out
and put inside a twelve year old boy,

who is now a grown man,
with two children, a wonderful wife,
and a bulldog named Brutus.

I wouldn't recognize
him on the street.

I pretend that some small part of my mother
lives on in him. I wonder what his arms hug like.

Today, I asked the truck stop clerk
if the coffee is fresh. He ignores me.

I pretend he has a bulldog named Brutus
and I laugh awkward as always.

He asks what was funny.
I ignore the question

and ask for cigarettes.

When you expect the worst, and are disappointed, you still lose.

I.

when the bent steel beams melt
the bend
becomes lost and irrelevant
becomes needed only for memories sake
becomes memory
becomes nothing
becomes no thing
becomes bent steel

II.

every clock
that has ever stopped
has the moment
of its first "tick"
behind its face.
that was a metaphor
about a friend's grandmother
succumbing to dementia
I explained it
because I wanted to explain
why we hide
we hide to stay safe
and that is a metaphor

I will not explain
nor should I have to.

III.
cars "whoooosh"
by my window
when I drive
I drive
in the slow lane
usually
usually
I am slower than them
they are faster than me
nicer than me
these cars I mean
newer
I should say

IV.
I have smoked weed
in the 48 contiguous states
and Hawaii
I did not do this on purpose

V.
the blue sky
reminds me

of my ex-wife's
dead body
I did not
see it in person
this dead body
that was once
my ex-wife
my daughter did
in my daughter's eyes
I see her dead mother
I do not wonder
why she never calls
I never call my father
I can hear him NOT saying
"your mother is dead"
everytime we speak

VI.

rivers are spiderwebs
when you see them
from the sky
they drape over land
the water
cuts
pulls the dirt
down into the seams
between ridges
spins in loops
zigs and zags

bounces higher
the glass lakes
either supply
or steal the water
it all depends
on where you look
the white ridges
jump to me
fall again
jump again
and so forth
until
the sea swallows

everything

swallows
everything

the sea swallows everything

THANKS TO:

Marissa, Travis, James, Hunter, Norah, and Alder (and Donny too).

Pop and all the family.
Swimming with Elephants Publications and all the family.

Beau, Ryan, Dylan, Amie, Billy, Candy, Carmendy, Ida, Maya, Larry, Adrienne, Anna, Julia, Nick, Alex, Mama, Ryk M, Jessie, Klark, Scottie, Shanna, Mike, Veda, Adam, Allie, Brennan, Brandon, Marty, Jen, Nate, PV, John, Richard Krech, Douglas, Thomas, Perry, Brecken, Jay, SaraEve, Cecily, AJ, Vogue, Mike, Caleb, Jaz, Vanessa in Canada, Rain City Slam, Loudmouth Slam, In One Ear, RichOak Alchemy Slam, Merc Slam, Ian, Paulie, Dre, Ashley, Liv, Theresa, Ryk, Mike, WORD Hum, Northtown Coffee, Jaime, Vidi, Mary, Jamey, Patrick, and Carrie, and rest well to my Mama, Grandaddy, Honeysun, Uncle Phil, Nano, Marci, Ricky, Uncle Robby, Gramma June, and all those we've lost.

Thank you to Great Weather for MEDIA, Swimming with Elephants Publications, Sargent Press, and Moon Pie Press for putting out my previous collections, and SwEP for doing it a 2nd time and hopefully in the future.

To my publisher and friend - Kat Crespin
A very extra thank you to Mary Holbrook, the best future mother in law that could be.

And also thanks to the authors whom I read and listened to while writing the bulk of the poems in this collection- Sharon Olds, Jessica Helen Lopez, Jack Micheline, Richard Krech, Matthew Dickman, Amie Zimmerman, Johnny Osi, Veda Leone, Vogue Robinson, Bill Moran.

(Photo by Greggory Deboor @ the Kurt Vonnegut Memorial Library)

Wil Gibson is a writer that currently lives in Humboldt County, California where the trees are big. He has had several collections published by kind people, and has been included in a number of anthologies and lit mags both online and in print. He has traveled across the country reading poems anywhere folks let him, has been on 7 National Poetry Slam teams from coast to coast, and would like to pet your dog and give you a hug, if you don't mind.

Find more info at wilgibson.com

Also available from
Swimming with Elephants Publications. LLC

Nail Gun and a Love Letter
Beau Williams

from below/ denied the light
Paulie Lipman

Cunt.Bomb.
Jessica Helen Lopez

September
Katrina K Guarascio & Gina Marselle

I Bloomed a Resistance from my Mouth
Mercedez Holtry

bliss in die/ unbinging the underglow
Sammy Bassam

Loved Always Tomorrow
Emily Bjustrom

Heartbreak Ridge and Other Poems
Bill Nevins

You Must Be This Tall to Ride
SaraEve Fermin

Swimming with Elephants
PUBLICATIONS

find these titles and many more at:
swimmingwithelephants.com

34509960R00078

Made in the USA
Middletown, DE
27 January 2019